Secrets of an Artist

by

Jenny Ray McGee

Secrets of an Artist

Follow on Instagram: livingonestepatatime

Acknowledgements

I want to say thank you to the people who have supported me in the journey of producing *Secrets of an Artist*. A special part of who I am is because of who you are, I love you all.

To my person, thank you for seeing my true colors. Even when I was broken, I would be so lost without you!

Jessica, thank you for seeing my words and helping me deliver them to others.

This book is dedicated to Zacoriyah Renee James

Always follow your dreams!!!

Table of Contents

Flowing

Flow from my fingertips the words I say.
Impact a person,
as they go about their day.
Reckon, beckon,
what the mind can do.

Inspire, inquire,
with the words, you speak.
Teach, by the things you display day to day.
Wisdom is knowledge, which turns into power.
Shower it.

Perspective.

The next step,
happens when you least expect it.

Lessons.
Samples of advice.
What people claim life should be.

Make them see.
What you want to be.
Let me breathe, rescue me.
From these labels thrown at me.

By people who cannot believe,
what it is to be a person like me.

Individuality.
Reality.
Expression.
As I expose, to them
every single part of who I am.

Duplicate

"Carbon copies of each other."
I turned abruptly and said to my mother.
"Why are they dressed, like one another?"
She answered with a smile instead.
Nodding her head.
Her expression read.
Do not be rude.
She communicated that with her attitude.
I huffed, knowing it was true.

Glancing up,
my eyes were met with a look of disgust.
Noses pointed up.
Their demeanor implied,
I am better than you.

In spite of speculation,
I held my head high.
As mother and I danced on by.

Can We Chat?

Articulation.
Will you catch?
Connection.
Conception.
Crumble.
Dilemma.
Acquire.
Love me, hate me.
Annihilate me.
Forsaken tragically.
Withstood. Exceptionally.

Secrets of an Artist

I have an artist sleeping in my soul.
Can you see her?
She lies next to the flowers, in the garden.
Waiting for her time to bloom.

Not till spring you see;
For winter must pass.

She smiles sleepily
I will wait patiently.
Slipping dormant silently.
Looking for a place to hibernate under these trees.

Time drips, slower than cold molasses.

I do not understand why she waits.
Continuing to sit, inactive.

Erupting in a sudden flash, it breaks.
The moment she has been waiting for!

Vibrant hues come crashing through
as the colors of my soul erupt free.
She leaps to her feet with glee.

Frolocking among the hues.
Shouting, *COME PLAY WITH ME*

Unleashing the magic within.
My soul burst into a grin.
Finally it is time my friend!

Courage

Be bold.

Do not always do what you are told.

Fight the fear that wants to take control,
it can and will paralyze you with its hold.
Life is a trip even when we fall, it requires us to stand tall.
Backing down is not allowed, I will stand out from the crowd.

I choose to let my voice be heard,
as passion drips from my words.
Believe in yourself.

Do not let doubt take over your life.
Live LIFE the way you say it should be.

Dreams are real.
Only killed when stifled from within.

Create moments, with the understanding
this could be my last day.
Live one step at a time.

As I Am

Simply complex. The way I like it best.
Smile at the smiley.
Contradiction, traditionally.

Take me as I am. Restless.
The best is yet to come.

I always take a stand, for what I believe in.
Try to understand. This is who I am.
Simply complex. The way I like it best.

Image

It is all about what people reflect to you.
A version of themselves. What they want you to see.

Like a shell, it creates such a space,
protecting one's soul, it is such a sacred place.
Allowing someone to be, who they want the world to see.
Unless it is used to fool us.

How do you decipher?
The ones, who are real
from those who are fake?

It is so hard to tell.

I often wonder.
Is everyone, just putting on an act?
Hiding who they truly are,
scared to embrace their true face.

An image can hold someone to the highest of standards,
then drop them down low.

We use it to judge.

Without taking the time to figure out; what is below?

When in reality an image,
is just that.

Something, imagined.

Speaking Through Me

Art and creativity exude from me.
Stamping out individuality and personality.
Appropriate for my soul!
As I walk a path alone.

Eclectic, electric.
Sparks fly.
I defy, tradition.

Listen.
All I can be.
The person I am; presently

Unique, I attempt to speak, independently.
From my mind and soul.
Imagination, the only way I unwind.

Inevitably I endeavor to accomplish the impossible.
Living my life fearlessly.
Chasing a dream drastically.
Holding onto my destiny!

My Piece of Peace

Where the lady of the land, meets the edge of the sea.
Where the sea aligns, with the infinite sky.
That's my spot of serenity.
A glimpse of beauty is all I need.
To cast me out of the darkness.
The sight of the ocean hurls me into reality.
Merciful to the movement.
Captivated by the moment.
I sit back, exhale.
Taking pleasure in this scene,
send me here for eternity.

A Form of Expression

You help to organize my thoughts.
So that I do not get lost.
Who would have guessed?
A blank page, pad, and pen.
Could heal the turmoil within.

Room for me to speak, in a world that is spoken.
Grabbing your undivided attention,
ensuring my words do not get broken.

Communication is key to the perception of me.

Dictating.
Respectfully.
Upholding a sense of vulnerability.

My complicated layers need plenty of space.
Grasping for air, in such a confined place.
With you, I create art, left open for interpretation.

Combining phrases accurately, forming the right imagery.
Accept the sounds that escape me.
Entirely.
Defining me through an art form,
literacy.

Note to Self

Trust yourself and decisions.
Thought process equals intuition.
Believe in your opinions.

Share often, so you are not forgotten.

Beware of chaos, for it will stab holes in your heart.
Facing adversity is hard.
Buck up and take charge.

Wear it as a badge, a battle won.
Character is discovered from the struggles we endure.

Fear not, when the heartbreak has passed.
The joyous feeling will last.

Honestly

Symphonic, symbolic sounds act as a distraction.
Silence leaves you with the wandering emptiness
of your thoughts.
Avoiding the hush of a deserted room acutely aware
hearing fears is a fatal attraction.
Granting permission for the mind to extract -
all the scenarios that leave your soul bruised and black.
Mental Russian roulette with; what thought will destroy
you next?
The mind sets a pace of panicking thoughts that race.
On a constant loop preparing for disaster, hoping for laughter.
The haunting thought of happiness lives in bliss- but not in the
world in which you exist

Free Spirit

Happiness is where I want to thrive, fulfilled on the inside.
Chasing purpose, living life make it worth it.
Carrying myself with pride.

Never looking back, with the thought; what have I done?
Instead of gazing forward, screaming, oh what fun.

I will take with me, consciousness.
Disregarding the palpable materialistic confines.

That is left behind, collecting dust

Once my spirit is free.
That my friend is no longer important to me.

Can I Have?

Can I have the pleasure of your company?
You had me with a single look,
through intense and shining eyes.

Would you like to go out with me?
To the movie or the park?
We could watch the sunset into the dark.

I want the pleasure of your company.
Will you tell me about yourself?
As we sit under the stars, surrounded by the moonlight.
On a beautiful and steamy summer night.

I am enjoying the pleasure of your company.
The most precious time, when we learn about each other.
Because we want to.
Listening intently as I reveal myself to you.
I love that part about you.
I hope we can continue to enjoy each other's company!

Space Between Us

A little goes a long way, at least that is what society says.
Although it is not applied today.

A sneer, a jeer flashes to those who are near.
Crude, rude,snot attitude.

To loved ones, strangers, friend or foe
Now it considered the norm to create a whirl-storm.
Acknowledged with a gesture.
Fake smiles and nods are excessive.

Do not be afraid to applaud others.
Only because.
If not to brighten a day.

Emote love,
verse hate.
Wouldn't that be great?!

Morning Light

Slipping into the dark I lose my senses.
Paralyzing and defenseless.
Fear comes in gripping waves
My beating heart pounding deviates.
"What happens in the dark?"
Something or someone stalks the night.
Lonely souls determined to create detriment.
Person or thing, laughs when you scream
Open your eyes, the voice whispers.
trickling down the air sending shivers
This is it, the time has come.
I open my eyes and am greeted by the morning sun.

To Know Me

To know me, means to know my heart.
For that is the most logical place to start.
I wear it on my sleeve you see, once hidden in the dark.

To know me, means to know my heart.
Love and laughter beats within the pulse, verifying, life still
matters.
It frowns, it stings, mainly it sings.

To know me, means to know my heart.
Compassion and empathy bleed from the seams,
sewn together, long before my name had a ring.

To know me, means to know my heart.
My mind is just as sharp.
Fearlessly guiding me,
I confide in it,
all of my secrets,
opening abundantly.
Repercussions be damned.
Wherever lies passion, it takes a stand.
Leading me aimlessly, to pursue,
 what is greater than my heart.
To invoke a bit of change.
It is the constant that remains.

To know me, is to know my heart.
Without a shadow of a doubt.
It carries the belief in who I am.
Countered negatively, with a furrowed brow,
By those, who do not understand or get me.

I stand with it,
by it,
for it,
because of it.

My heart tells me what to do.

To know me, means to know my heart.
It is the fire that breathes this life in me, not only metaphorically.
It took a while to trust it, hell yeah it has fucking busted.
Fighting against it for no other reason than, because.
Influences shaping it momentarily,
into something I am not.
A conformist,
A follower,
Shaping me to fit in.
One more time as loud as you can,
I am who I am.

Compartments of me will always have room to grow.
Morphing into the best I can be, I would not change it for the
world.
The demon I rebelled against the most, was the one who remained
close.
Never giving up or giving in.
To know me, is to know my heart- for it is the most logical place to
start!

Flying

Free, like a cool breeze.
My spirit is restless, leaving me breathless.

Roaming to uncover adventure.
I feel chained to fences.
Defenseless.
Stepping into the world.
Alone, Crippling.

Do not let your gumption die.
Inhale courage. Absorb it.

Overlook the no, blaze the yes.
Shatter boundaries.
Try your best.

Failure, not having enough bravery to try.

Stillness

Empty space lurks across.
Shadows prowl, in every nook.
Darkness looms, causing my heart to boom.
Beating faster, against my skin.

Stop.

Take a deep breath in.
Shhhhh silence.
Shhhhh be quiet.

You Left

I thought I had forever.
Then it was goodbye.
You went too soon.
In the blink of an eye.
I did not see it coming.

It was so unexpected.
I never said my final goodbye.
It hurt like hell.
The pain inside.
My heart was broken.
I just cried.

It hit me to the depths.
I struggled with the concept,
death.

I was not prepared for
such a feeling
loss.

A piece of me
left, with you.
That cannot be replaced.
Instead.
I stare at pictures of your smiling face.

You taught me hard lessons.
I am sorry for the times.
I was not listening.
I will admit most of them did not sink in
the moment you taught them.
Now I carry them forever in all that I do.
For that, I need to say thank you.

You helped to shape me into the person I am.
You were my best friend.

I know you loved me,
this is no doubt.
To the moon and back, I want to shout.

I miss you always,
and think of you often.
All though it was long ago,
you are not forgotten.

Welcomed, Like a Spring Rain

I learned to embrace change;
like an unannounced spring rain.
Arriving abruptly, dissipating instantaneously.
Leaving traces behind, only when inspected carefully.

Popping up, some remark, just my luck.

I make the most out of change,
similar to jumping among the rain.
Never bothering to take note of
what's happening to my clothes

Love nature, for what we need.
Life, so we can breathe.
Splashing in puddles, kicking up droplets.
Do not knock it.
The shower will pass, sometimes with a storm.
Flowing like the river, bobbing in the current.
No longer fighting, what is outside of my control.

JUST ME

My words will not be left unspoken.
My heart will be left open.
I commit to keep growing.
My mind will not sit in waste,
nor will my dreams be left to chase.

Continuing to push myself outside,
past my safe place.
I will not be caught, stopped,
or told to ponder.
I will try to never
permit myself to be left wondering;
what could have been?
Promising myself to attempt every opportunity.
Hesitation means,
missing moments.
Vanished.

My voice will be heard,
if only by me.
I will listen.
I am worth it.

I speak, articulately about what I need.
Clearly. So as not to cloud.
I am direct. As I shout above the crowd.
Happiness and peace
is what I seek.
If only for myself.

What Happens in the Dark?

*My love is in the shape of a
fist.*
Imprinted with every strike.
Do not fight.
It will be worse for you.

*Your actions forced me into
this.*
Mind your place,
GET OUT OF MY FACE
I say with a glare.
If you run, I will find you.
Duck, dive or hide;
*I have control and will not let
it slide.*

We are not equal,
you lost that right.
*From the moment you
stepped on my floor.*
*Yes, I have the right to call
you a whore.*
Disconnected, from those
who kept you protected.

No more.

Turn to me, after the pain.
I will explain,
what you did to deserve this.
My fist.
As I pick you up off the floor.

Do as you are told.
Be near me.
Fear me.
Come when I call.

*I am the drug you cannot
quit.*
Addicted.
I have got your fix.
Quick.
There is no end.
I am not done, having fun.
Save me.

Dad

Keep avoiding your own healing.
I never meant to hurt anyone but me.

Anger boils, from within.
Drowning, living in sin, according to you.

Judging from a point of view in which you do not see the real me.
You've buried me by the impression you've formed, scorned.
By your outside unwanted opinions.

Refusal to expand your mind,
rewinding what has occurred between you and me.
I cannot change what you believe,
I can continue, being a better version of me.
I know you do not accept me.

Your approval means nothing to me.
Go back up the tree,
far away from me,
as you look down and frown,
on who I choose to be.
You're missing out, not me.

Love and Light

Love and light shine bright,
from within my soul.
Shape and mold me into the person I am supposed to be.
Show me.
Whenever, I veer off track, quickly and lovingly pull me back.
Never criticizing allowing, me to mark out my own path.

Love and light shine bright.
I choose you, you are my path.
Fill my heart,even in the darkest parts.
Take hold.
Love and light shine bright.

Romancing Creativity

Sing and dance, trying to romance my creativity.
This artist, who wants to explode from me.
Released from the core of my life.
Soul contract
Casually dragging me up the currents passing by.
Going against the stream.
Pushing me to live my dream.
I watch in awe.
I trust the universe and its plan.
Leading me fearlessly, to carve out my space.
Which identifies me, in the race. To build something special,
never seen before.
That something.
Me.

Cascading

Curls from the tip sticks a moment in time.
Leaping from the mass, briefly it lasts.
Cascading on a dime.
Weeping in the abyss it mists.
Winding back in time. Rewind.
Something previously existing.
Listen to the thunderous sounds. Thrashing all around.
Splits, colors burst.
Blue, green and white.
Such a sight.
My eyes behold before me.
Crashing by my side, as I reside with the tide.
Floating right next to me.

A Pure Heart

The innocence of a child;
reveals the purest of hearts.
Yet to be tainted.

Viewing life through wanderlust eyes,
curiosity engulfs them, like a flame.

New discoveries, uncovered.
Greeted with a smile.
Without expectations, of good, or evil.

Toxify their minds, quickly.
Set an example of hate.

Teaching them to relate: skin color,
gender,
life patterns,
path and purpose,
with a negative connotation.

Steaming from,
a lack of understanding.
Fueled by fear.

Afraid of those who,
look and act differently.
Tricking us to judge,
based off of labels.

Developed by a system, they cash in.
Placed above, better than the rest. Materially.

Feeding the blame,
pointing at each other.

Instead of fixing and loving,
ourselves and another.

New Life

Bonded by
a connection created.
You are part of me.
Forever.
Till the end.
Gifted to protect.

Guiding you through,
the things I have learned.
Attempting, to prevent.
The painful lessons of life.

Unsuccessful.

Keeping a close eye on you.
Thank you for letting me,
observe your journey.
From a safe distance.

Coaching when you trip.
Intending.
I see you in me.
Imprinting.

When you smile,
I smile.
Your tears are mine.
I am your mother and friend.
I will stand by you, till the end.

Adversity

Why are you always stressing
me?

Placing that pressure down
on me.
Crushing my spirit like it has
to be.
Done in the right way,
like you say,
it needs to be.

Why are you always stressing
me?
Asking questions, so I have
to be.
Suffocated to a plan, because
"that is how it should be."

Why are you always stressing
me?
Demanding money.
Taking something.
You say I owe.
Contractually.
Circumstances change
drastically.
Simply for breathing this life
in me.
Existing dramatically.
Refusing to play radically.
I hate that you are always
stressing me!

Why are you always stressing
me?
Sit back.
Relax.
Enjoy life, how it can be.

Will you stop stressing me?
Absurd.
Have you not heard?
This is life, you see.
A bunch of adversity.
Trips, bumbles, and stumbles.
To overcome.
You will never be done.
Facing and replacing one
with the next.
Tackle it the best, way you
please.

What you perceive as stress,
is love from me.
I want everything for you.
You worry me.
Still I am cheering,
but I am leery.
This is scary.

No biggie I get it.
But I refuse to quit.
What I am seeking you will
see!

Pills

Take this.
Go on swallow that.
Don't you dare, ask why!

Fact.
We are keeping you alive.
Nothing else matters.

I counter with a sigh.

Dive further away,
from the truth.
what is real?

THE POWER OF WILL

Determination and pride.
Watch me, stay alive.

AS I DIE

The odds are against me.

I fight fire with fire.
Light a match.
Give up, give in
I would, if I could.
But my mind will not let me.

Start from the beginning, breath.
Be at ease.

I am living one step at a time.
Nothing changes quickly!
Not on your dime.

I AM RUNNING OUT OF TIME

CRY! SCREAM! SPIT.
QUIT.

Poking and prodding at me.

I do not want your help, but I need it.

Contradiction at best.
Time to rest.

LEAVE ME ALONE!!!
I want to go home.
I plea.
As a deafening silence,
surrounds me.

I already know the no,
before spoken.

The beats of my heart,
pulse in the back.
As the medicine attacks.
As it slowly kills.
Contradiction at best.
Trickle, trickle, drip, drip
into the vein.

You drive me insane.

I will survive and thrive,
from the foundation you gave me.
Trust is earned, not commanded.

You left me stranded.
You are not forgiven.

Answer my question,
as I approach.
Do you think my life is a joke?

Grasp

It is out of my reach.
Right there at the end,
Everything I want.
I could begin, again.

Hold on.
Can I not touch it?

Grasp,
within my fingertips.
I try.
It slips.
Eludes.

Fed up with the process.
I do not know what to do.

Silence.
I stare.
It is right there.

Desperation.
I use all my might,
grab.

Miss.
With disappointment.
As I lose my breath.

It has disappeared.
Gone in an instant.
Into the past.
Leaving behind nothing left to grasp!

Screams

I am my own worst enemy. Self-destruct every entity.
Creating personal demise.
Self-detrimental and demeaning always screaming,
on the inside.
Cutting away little pieces with no remorse.

Tracks in my brain, stating, no.
You cannot. You're not good enough.
Stop.

I am my own worst enemy.
Walls go up, hiding from the hurt.

As I slap on a smile and crank up the dial,
cruising down the path called life.

Self-loathing, never knowing if the pain will end.

I wish I could see the beauty in me.
Do not be vain,
it is not good to gloat.

Hold your head high,
do not be a snob.
Have an attitude,
without being crude.
With all these societal rules,
I cannot find my niche.
Blaming and shaming myself,
with every step I take.

I will not look in the mirror and face the reflection I see.
The one staring back at me and I hate.
Who I have allowed myself to be.

I do not know the woman staring back at me.
I am my own worst enemy.

Motion

Tidal waves, come float me away.
Sailing current, from night to day.
My spirit takes flight.
With open eyes above the clouds.
I will be loud.
Splashing around, joyously.

Tidal waves, come float me away.
So that I may drift in the sunset.

Enjoying the end and beginning of each day.
Lapping in the warmth between basking and relaxing.
Oh, deep blue.

Tidal waves, come float me away.
So I may swim within,the creatures, living off the bay.
Winding through salty seas. They would take the lead,
I follow along happily.
Nature as far as the eye can sea.
Ocean Basin.
Tidal waves, come float me away.

Blinded

Blinded by what cannot be seen,
Everything is so new.
Swept out of reality.
Discarding the known.
Slowly letting go escaping, draping, forming.
Grow.
Articles of expansion, articulation of evolution.
Push through. Step.
Comfort, the reason we compress.
Cease and decrease the walls you've built.
Playing face, to the space that reflects back.
Shrugging towards the judging, paying no mind.
Dare to evaluate; how much can relate?
When you look in, the only place to begin.

Nothing To Do

Sitting around thinking my mind drifts to you.
You have no idea what it is that you do.
In fact, that is the reason I am attracted to you.

Filling my heart with delight, you make it dance,
like the fire, on a dark and snowy night.

This is so very new, however I cannot wait to see,
the possibilities I find with you!

You have been hurt, I can see it in your eyes.
I am not here to do that, I say with a sigh.
I swear not to clog your brain with lies.

Winning your trust, with every topic we discuss,
waiting for the moment you let me in.
Enough to meet your kin?

You bring out the best in me,and are learning to deal with the rest
of me.
I love it when you call my name. Drawing me near as it soothes.

Sitting around thinking my mind wanders to you.
You have no idea what it is that you do.

The Call

Helpless I watch as it drifts astray.
Slipping further and further away;
closing doors as it tucks, stuck.

Clinging to familiarity instead.
Jump forth damn it, towards the unknown.
You coward, you chicken.
Afraid to be alone.

Chase after, faster.
Pause only for a moment.
Leap without fear.
Never let up, my dear.

Relying on fate,
a safety net?
You will not regret it.

Caught up in the rhythm,
in place of a new beginning.
Forgiven.

Opportunities missed.
Fades in the abyss.
Gone in a flash.
Dash.
Capture, make the instant last.

Catch.
What belongs to you?
The one thing that matters.
Do not be ashamed.
Remain,
for when you reach the top of life's game.
It is worth every amount of pain.

Interlocking

Your touch makes me shiver.

Whenever you are near,
my knees start to quiver.
I look into your eyes,
and know it will be alright.

My heart rapidly beats,
when you smile ear to ear.
I am so happy and lucky,
to be laying next to you here.
My dear.

Some say I give my heart, drastically.
I call it passionately.
Do you care,
to know it?
As I show it,
to you.

I will leave it bare.
Please place my heart in a safe place.

Inner lock it with yours?

As we explore,
turning two souls to one,
the magic has begun.
Come take me there.

Holes

I feel honored,
you took a page from my
book.
Imitation is the highest form
of flattery.

Sadly he does not know.
Actions speak louder than
words. Reaction.
Shows you care,
Without emotions, you would
not dare.

You lost. It is a shame we
must play these games.
Spite is still an action.
That my friend, is a fact son.
It shows that you are broken.
By the things I have done.

Shunned from your heart and
mind.
Rewind.
You wear a mask.
Pretending.
Like life is not ending.
Hiding.
Such a shame.
high society.
Acting like everyone should

worship thee.
What have you done?
Clearly.
You are not the man you
claim to be.
Plain to see.
As if you are playing me.
Closed off.

Take a shot.
I invented that foolery.
Sincerely,
I used you just as much as
you used me.
For a void, I do not want to
fill.

Take that shit the other way.
Sucker punch, to the gut?

The fear of losing, ought to
be,
The key to what is blocking
me.
I wait patiently.
Flaws and all.
For what?
Not you.

Forgotten

How, when and where, did we allow this to happen?!
A beautiful soul left in the cold.
Turns frozen and rotten.
Freeze time and stop it.
Broken pieces, shattered around.
Quickly bending down.
Gathered with care.
Be safe.
The time has begun.
Unravel and reveal,
secrets and scars.
Pouring darkness into light.
Let healing take flight,
come to a place we share.

Tragedy

Pain turns to anger which screams inside.
Not at any time, willing to let up and die.
Internally bleeding. Let me breathe again.

Yanking back tragedy.
Why is this anger always mad at me?
Burrowing deep like a planted seed.
I want LIFE to come back for me!

Abandoned by the sadness, negativity, surrounding me.
What? I do not want to see.
What? Stares right back at me.

Mocking me, stalking me.
Hopelessly spitting at me.
Trying to overtake.
My heart aches.

The Other Half

You are a silent killer.
It is such a crazy game you play.
You do not care. Striking every single day.
No one can predict which victim you will pick.
A numbers game.
I guess.
You do understand,
the damage you have done.
To friends, families and even myself.
The impact is felt.

Days spent stuck in bed,
each passing second,
wishing to be dead.

Some you haunt for years at a time.
Others you take so fast,
it is a crime.

The worst part about you,
doctors cannot predict,
which family members you will miss,
verse the ones you will get.

What sucks even more,
is never being explained.
To the patients and parents,
looking for someone to blame.

You sentence people, to a life of pain.

Wheelchairs and braces.
Some of them you maim.

I look around; this is really true?
Glancing in the mirror, all I see is you.
Do you realize the agony you put me through?!

Hazy Days

Darkness creeps in, winding through the brain.
Keeping a tight leash, taunting relentlessly.
Ever so sneakily.
Suggesting, you belong to me.

Darkness creeps in, playing mind games.
Repeating and cheating, the progress being made.
Since the last time, in a past time,
when it appeared.

Darkness creeps in, screaming, teasing, coxing.
To keep you broken.

Darkness creeps in, silently, violently, whispering.
You are alone.

In the depths of your despair.
Clinging on, telling you wrong.

You are not stuck here.
Mentally, physically, spiritually.
robbing you bare.

Darkness creeps in, sucking the life from your soul.
As you allow it, to crowd your mind.

Broken

United as a whole.
The lie being told.
Stand up and face it.
Do not just lay there being complacent.
What is wrong with you?!
Why will you not change it?!
With a straight face, you have the audacity to say.
Everything is fine, it will be okay.
Look around, said with a frown.
We are going to go down.
Trumpets marching, blaring that sound.
Living in ignorant bliss.
Wake up I plead, stop avoiding me.
Too late. Watch and wait.
Damage, Destruction.
All for nothing.
This is more than I can bare!

Shipwreck

Frozen in a moment,
I am left broken.
Scattered pieces all around.
I lay in wait.
Fighting the urge to run and hide.
Exposed to the sky.
Cleaning up wreckage.
I hear no sound.
Except the voices in my head.
And they beg.
Surrounding.
Screaming. Release me free.
My spirit haunts me.
Daunting.
I am lost and forgotten.
Who cares, I'm rotten.

41

Violation

Discrimination is a violation,
of who I am.
Extraordinary.

You judge me.
Off skin,
complexion.

You have got to be kidding me.
You are not.
I stop.

As you pass, by.
With judgment.
I sigh.
Sadly.

Standing behind a nation,
relaying a message to the generation, below.
It is okay to hate.

REEVALUATE.

The actions you display,
through emotion and the notion.
Saying "everything is okay."

Accepting negativity,
as a replacement for change.

YOU.
SHOULD.
BE.
ASHAMED.

About the Artist

My name is JennyRay McGee, thank you for exploring my first book of poetry with me. Poetry is my first love, as a young woman I found inspiration by reading poets such as Langston Hughes, Walt Whitman and Emily Dickinson. Intrigued by the way their words painted a picture in my mind, I was transported to a magical space, sitting amongst the shelves of my hometown library.

When I was a little girl I started writing poems as a way to cope with the life-threatening medical condition my body suffered from. I found expressing my inner turmoil through writing to be the only way I could heal.

Holding onto the dream of being considered a writer and author, I compiled *Secrets of an Artist* over a two year period. Transforming myself from a shy, timid, dreamer into a full blown literature artist.

Follow On Instagram: Livingonestepatatime

***

Made in the USA
Middletown, DE
02 May 2021

38240774R00024